01

Setting out on the journey to define your business, Handbook 02 of 'Launch Your Own Successful Creative Business' will help you explore the foundations and drivers for your activities. These are the building blocks that will help shape your business for the future.

Business Facts
Do you have a good idea or a good business idea

Intellectual Property
How to identify, protect and exploit your IP

Values
Identifying the values that underpin your activities

Mission Statement
Summarise the impact you want to make with your business

Evidence
Using evidence modelling and future evidence, illustrate what success will look like for you.

www.nesta.org.uk

02

BUSINESS FACTS

There are two questions that anyone setting up a business needs to be able to answer at the drop of a hat:

- **What is it that I do?**
- **Why should my customers care?**

Take a moment to write a short sentence that encapsulates what it is you do. Then another saying why that should matter to your customers. This is known as an 'elevator pitch'. Keeping it concise can be tricky. If you find yourself waffling on, keep refining your words until you have something short and to the point. Your answers might look something like this:

What is it that I do?
I run a service design company.

Why should my customers care?
Because I offer a creative service that makes my customers' products more appealing, and means they sell more.

To examine these two questions a little deeper, here are some basic business facts that you must take on board.

01   Customers have to want what you're offering

A business needs income to survive, and income is based on the demand for your product or service. Market research can help you to find out if there is a demand, or the potential for it. On page 05 we talk more about spotting demand opportunities.

02   You need to say how you meet that demand

You'll have to describe how your product or service will meet those needs. Talk about the benefits it will bring, rather than describing its features and functions. You can check the benefits through customer satisfaction surveys. Remember, you'll want customers to come back, so it's important to listen to their needs.

03 You have to keep appealing to that demand

Even when you know a demand exists, and you've made your appeal to it, you can't rest. Customer demand is like putting petrol in a car. You may be going along, even at speed, but unless you keep refuelling you'll grind to a halt at some point. You can 'refuel' by developing a sales and marketing plan that concentrates on acquiring customers.

04 You have to continuously innovate to compete and survive

This is done through a competitive strategy. Five guiding principles make the difference and help ensure a business is focussed, productive and ultimately successful:

01 You're not at the centre of your idea, your customers are.

02 You don't need to do everything yourself. Build partnerships and alliances.

03 You need a vision for your business in order to position your offering. And you need to communicate this vision clearly and consistently.

04 You need to understand your personal motivation for running a business, including the importance of financial returns.

05 You need to be able to measure the performance of your business, which at certain critical moments can only be measured in terms of money.

These facts are the basis for everything that follows. If your business idea doesn't stack up against them, then you should seriously question whether it's likely to work.

A GREAT IDEA OR A GREAT BUSINESS IDEA?

An idea tends to have your thoughts and desires as its focus. But a business idea needs to have customers, clients or audience as its focus. Three key facts distinguish a business idea from a creative idea:

01 There must be a clear need for your product or service (or you must create one), and you should be providing a new or improved solution for that need.

02 That need must have sufficient potential to create a demand.

03 There should be sufficient reward within your idea to be able to support your immediate business needs, as well as your future business requirements.

Product Example: Dyson

Inventor James Dyson introduced the bagless vacuum cleaner that promised greater suction than conventional vacuums and so cleaner carpets. Enough people were dissatisfied with their current vacuum cleaners to create demand for the new Dysons. The company's reward was that it made enough money not just to break even, but to extend its range of vacuum cleaners and diversify into other products.

Service Example: Easyjet

Easyjet was key to revolutionising air travel by making it affordable. The company set up in 1995 with two aircraft offering low cost air fares by providing a core service and charging for extras like hold baggage and food. Consumer demand has fuelled the success of the company. Its reward is that it is now one of the largest airlines in Europe and was floated on the London Stock Exchange in 2000.

05

Spotting Opportunities

Having an innovative product or service can open markets where none existed before challenging the existing competitive landscape. It allows you to build a new monopoly (even if just for a short while), which will allow you to grow without competition. But be careful! Innovators who are first to market often have negative experiences and lose money, while followers reap the rewards: benefiting from awareness of the product or service, and introducing revised versions that iron out teething problems and avoid intellectual property issues.

So alongside the questions 'What is it that I do?' and 'Why should my customers care?', you should ask yourself:

- Is there a need for what I'm offering?
- Will there be sufficient demand?
- Will that generate sufficient reward for me to move my business forward?

What is Intellectual Property?[1]

If you've spotted an opportunity or thought of an idea, you need to think about Intellectual Property.

Music. Books. Computer software. Products we use in our daily lives… each is a product of human creativity, and that creativity is protected. It is creations of the mind, once expressed, that make up intellectual property (IP).

The crucial word here is "expressed". There's no IP protection in the UK for ideas or concepts, only for expression of those ideas or concepts.

1: Original content by Own-it, intellectual property advice for creative businesses

06

A GREAT IDEA OR A GREAT BUSINESS IDEA?

The most common types of IP protection for certain types of activities are:

- **Patents and Design Rights /** technical solutions, new inventions and products
- **Copyright /** for literary, artistic, dramatic and musical works
- **Trade Marks /** for brand names, words, sounds and even (very rarely) smells.

In business, everything from your own designs, software, brand, packaging and logo should be protected. In a nutshell, all of your mental and creative outputs can be transformed into tangible commodities so that you can license, sell, trade, divide or retain your rights to those commodities.

It is important to consider how you can protect, exploit and manage your intellectual property effectively.

Managing Your IP and Unlocking the Value of Your Creativity

Some of what follows may be for later down the line in the development of your business, but it's worth being aware of it now.

Step 1 – Identify Your Intellectual Property

- List your creative assets (your IP) including your logo and company name/brand, packaging design, products and software.
- Check your designs, expressed ideas, concepts and creative works are new and original.

Step 2 – Protect Your Intellectual Property

- Have a simple confidentiality agreement that you use with clients, potential manufacturers or investors BEFORE you start negotiations.

- Register designs, patents and trademarks at the UK Intellectual Property Office website.

- Secure internet domain names to safeguard your brand.

- When approaching manufacturers get agreement terms in writing such as confidentiality agreement, prototype agreement (whereby the factory agrees to make a sample to your specifications), heads of agreement and manufacturing agreement.

- Keep good records including work in progress. This includes your sketches, notes, drafts, diagrams, contracts, letters and email communications.

- Mark the author/publisher or creator's name on all copies of your work, along with the date and country. © (Name of owner) (Year of creation).

- Put registered design rights and other IP renewal dates in your diary. Never forget IP rights or domain name renewals.

Step 3 – Exploit Your Intellectual Property

- Ensure any designs, trademarks and patents you register or apply for are the same as those you intend to market.

- Put your design rights number on any packaging and ® if you have a registered trademark to enhance your profile.

- Maximise returns by licensing your rights either as a whole or separately to exploit your IP in different territories or different forms – this way you hold onto your rights whilst making money from them.

- Charge an assignment fee if the client wants the rights, always seek external advice before assignment.

08

A GREAT IDEA OR A GREAT BUSINESS IDEA?

- License your IP (either exclusively or non-exclusively). You can license your rights exclusively to the licensee only, or non-exclusively to the licensee and anyone else you choose to license to. You can license reproduction or distribution rights, rental or lending rights. Consider what you are licensing (e.g. your trademark, copyright, design rights) in what format (exclusively or non-exclusively) and how long for (e.g. are the terms of the licence for a fixed term, perpetual or terminal) and finally, where in the world you are licensing to?

- Figure out whether you require royalties, licence fees or both. (Royalty payments generally vary between 4 and 14%, dependent on the type of creative work/industry).

- Negotiate fair terms. This is the period where you spend time bargaining to work out a deal. Next comes the contracting part, which involves formulating the details to create a binding agreement.

- Make sure you are given equitable remuneration for your work. For example if you produce sound recordings, you should be paid royalties. If you have written a book, you should receive lending royalties as well as royalties from your publisher.

- Use a Creative Commons licence if you want to control and share your IP. You can choose to allow reproductions of your work but not for commercial purposes or other methods of use, so some rights are reserved instead of all.

Step 4 – Enforce Your Intellectual Property

Even large organisations can experience problems enforcing their IP. DVD piracy costs the film industry hugely, just as illegal music downloading costs the music industry. So how can you enforce your IP effectively?

– Monitor what competitors and new entrants to your market are doing. Get news alerts, subscribe to industry news, keep an eye on the UK Intellectual Property Office site and pay attention to new trademarks being advertised. If any infringe yours you are able to contest them once they've been advertised.

– Send standard cease and desist letters if you find anyone infringing your IP rights. A lawyer can help draw up an effective letter to send out and advise you on the best course of action.

More information on identifying, protecting and maximising your IP can be found through organisations including Own-it: Intellectual Property Advice for Creative Businesses.

10

VALUES

Values

When you're running your own business, you are in control. You decide what you work on. You have the opportunity to create a business that is as you want it to be – a venture that truly reflects your own enthusiasm, passion and values.

While profitability is vital for any business to be able to survive and prosper, it is essential that you align your business and how you run it with your personal values. These are not necessarily morals or ethics, but simply the things that make you feel truly alive and passionately committed to what you're doing. For one person it might be service to others; for another it might be creativity or innovation; and for someone else it might be travel, adventure or discovery.

You will have a greater sense of energy, commitment and enthusiasm for starting, developing and running a business that is aligned with your values. It will give you greater determination and resourcefulness in getting over the difficulties and challenges of setting up a business and maintaining it.

Your values will affect a number of areas: how you work, how you wish your work to be received and how you interact with customers, suppliers and funders.

> "Though I found it hard to come up with the values under pressure, just realising that I should think about my business in relation to my values was a lesson I will take into the future."

Tom Dowding, Mobile Content Designer, Mobile Pie

Values are different from beliefs. Abi Yardimci, Creative Education Specialist and writer explains:

"The difference between a belief and a value (for me) is that a value is something you hold very dear, like something precious that you protect against all odds to keep intact. A belief is something that underpins your actions and your direction in life. Beliefs can change, and when they do you see big shifts in energy, emotion and attitude…"

Use Worksheet 02a: Your Values[1] to help you identify and prioritise your values and build them into your plans for your business. On your stickies write down the values that are important to you. The table on the next page has a list of possible values to get you started.

---

1. This exercise has been adapted from content provided by business advisor, Joanna Woodford.

www.nesta.org.uk

12

VALUES

Then prioritise those you've selected and arrange them into the relevant columns on Worksheet 02a. Try to have a maximum of five values in the 'Always Important' column.

Achievement	Personal development	Respect
Advancement and promotion	Meaningful work	Harmony
Influencing others	Money	Aesthetics
Independence	Power and authority	Humour
Honesty	Public service	Work life balance
Helping society	Quality of what I take part in	Excitement
Helping other people	Recognition	Excellence
Growth	Reputation	Economic security
Financial gain	Supervising others	Decisiveness
Fame	Status	Ecological awareness
Integrity	Stability	Creativity
Innovation	Self respect	Co-operation
Market position	Responsibility and accountability	Competition
Leadership	Time freedom	Community
Knowledge	Wisdom	Competence
Job tranquillity	Work under pressure	Change and variety
Intellectual status	Work with others	Challenging problems
Physical challenge	Working alone	Art
Freedom		

Getting off the ground   How to go about setting up a creative business

Why are Values Important?

Now that you've named your values, you'll be able to use them in a number of ways. Think of them as a kind of radar to scan your work and the other areas of your life, and notice which things are creating a real sense of fulfilment and excitement (and equally, which are not).

They'll help you to:

- Assess your business idea in terms of how it honours your values.
- Test how your work/life balance needs to be adjusted.
- Stay inspired when dealing with the more mundane aspects of business or when things aren't going so well.
- Keep on track when you're offered different choices or opportunities. For example, what happens if you're short of cash and are offered some work that doesn't really fit in with your plan?
- Communicate why someone should care about your business, as your values often connect with those held by other people.

It's possible that there'll be tension between your personal values and your business values. For example, you may not care about money, but making a profit is essential to building a sustainable business. So how do you use your personal values to inspire, guide and shape your business? One way is to look at the various aspects of being in business, and to think about which of your values is most important to each aspect.

14

VALUES

Your values are also vital in building a brand and have to be consistent with your actions. If you act in a way that conflicts with the values that your customers understand this could have significant consequences and even result in a backlash. This was the case with Innocent Drinks, who recently struck a deal with Coca Cola.

Innocent brand

Innocent, founded 10 years ago and fêted for its healthy drinks and ethics – it donates 10% of profits to charity – provoked a vitriolic outpouring from scores of customers when Coca-Cola took a share in the company. As far as they were concerned, the firm might as well have done a deal with the devil. One railed: "You have sold your soul. That's the last time we buy your produce." Others lamented the end of the fairy tale: "No more jolly blogs, cutie e-mails, cottage-industry-style village fetes or sweetie messages on the side of cartons please… they just don't fit with your brand image anymore."

They [Innocent's founders] also appear to be blinkered to the apparent conflict between what Innocent purportedly stands for – health and social values – and Coca-Cola's position as one of the flagbearers of global capitalism.

(Source: business.timesonline.co.uk)

WHAT'S YOUR BUSINESS DRIVEN BY?

To be successful, you need to balance your drive to develop your idea into a business with other imperatives.

If an enterprise is primarily driven by ideas but doesn't have a commercial aspect, it won't be sustainable. Similarly, if a business is motivated by commercial imperatives without due consideration to its innovation and creativity, then it may not be effective in the long-term. Achieving a balance between passions, talents and economic drive is important.

> "Thinking about myself, my ideals, my motivations and the impact of my business was much more valuable to me than simply knowing how a business functions."

Holly McIntyre, Online Recruitment for Creative Practitioners

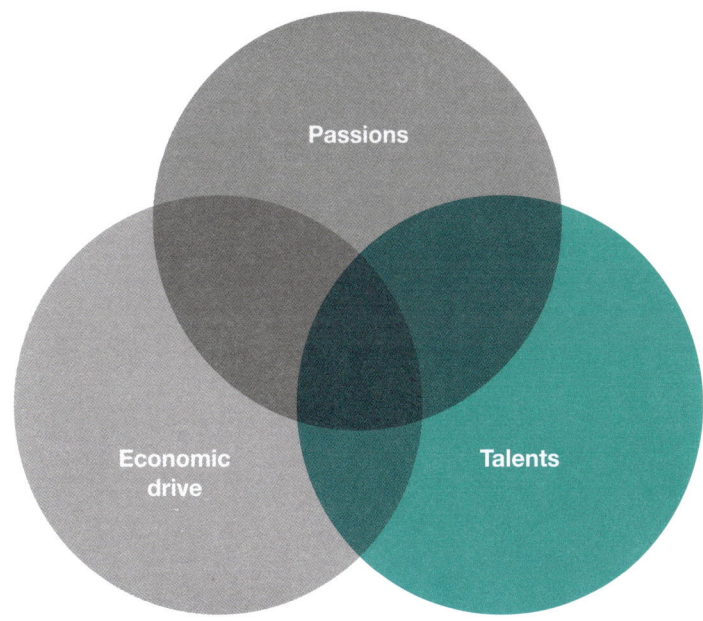

16

WHAT'S YOUR BUSINESS DRIVEN BY?

The illustration on page 15 is developed from 'Good to Great' by Jim Collins. Collins studied the qualities and drivers that distinguished great companies. Excellent companies are focussed on activities that ignite their passions, fully utilise their skills and talents, and have clear insight into how to most effectively generate sustained and robust cash flow and profitability.

It's probably easiest to identify what your passions are. Many will have been outlined in your values. This handbook will help you to weigh each of the drivers against the skills needed to take your idea forward, and the financial efficiency of what you're proposing.

Mission Statement

Having broadly explored your idea as a business proposition, the values that will underpin it and the drivers for your activities, you can now draft a mission statement.

A mission statement is a clear, concise summary of why a business exists and its future intentions. A mission statement can tell customers a lot about your business, so it's very important to take time to develop it. Have a look at some other companies' mission statements for guidance.

Ideally the mission statement should be motivational, realistic and only 3-4 sentences long. It should be similar to an executive summary stating what your company is, what you do, what your business intentions are and why you are in business. Virgin Atlantic's mission statement is:

To grow a profitable airline where people love to fly and where people love to work.

EVIDENCE MODELLING

Determining a vision for you and your business is usually a simple task for an entrepreneur. You have an idea in mind that you're passionate about, and you're determined to make happen. But can you articulate that vision? Can you describe it or draw it, and above all do you understand how your vision might take shape as a business?

There's a process called Evidence Modelling that can help you explore these questions. It's based on research by Marshall McLuhan. Being an academic, he came up with the 'Tetrad of Media Effects', which sounds more complex than it actually is. Basically, it poses four questions you can run your idea past:

01 What does it enhance?

02 What does it replace/make less desirable?
For example, online news – with blogs and so on – is making the traditional newspaper less desirable.

03 What does it revive?
New ideas can change how we see and value older ones. For example, because people now mostly buy music digitally, vinyl records have changed from being common to being rare. And that means they now have a new value as collectible objects worth a lot of money.

04 What might be the backlash?
Could an idea become so successful it actually ends up having a negative effect? For example, if a car-sharing service is so well designed it actually tempts people off public transport and into cars, increasing congestion, then a successful idea actually ends up having a negative effect.

18

EVIDENCE MODELLING

Evidence Modelling is helpful to illustrate the extremes of success as experienced by Burberry.

Burberry brand

Burberry became famous for a remarkable brand repositioning at the end of the 1990s. Established for 150 years, it was closely associated with the British upper class by virtue of its iconic trench coat and check pattern. By the 1980s the popularity of the brand was waning and it was failing to find favour with new generations. Profits fell from £37m to £25m in 1997. A new CEO, Rose Marie Bravo, was recruited to overhaul the brand. She appointed new designers who updated the clothing range and developed new products. A new advertising campaign was launched using celebrities like Kate Moss, who became the face of the product.

Burberry was trying to retain its core values of quality and exclusivity whilst giving them a modern appeal. New stores were opened and unprofitable ones closed, and accessories and gifts were promoted as part of the new strategy. In 2005 the company's profits had risen six fold. One of the downsides of this was the adoption of the brand by unsavoury types and a social group known as 'chavs', as well as a flood of counterfeit goods. Burberry responded by acting against counterfeiters and by reducing the use of the ubiquitous check and stopping selling Burberry caps.

What did the overhaul enhance?
- brand prominence and recognition
- use of check as status symbol

What did it replace/make less desirable?
- high-end product becomes mainstream, losing its exclusivity

What did it revive?
- new demand for check
- new demand for older style product now seen as fashionable

What was the backlash?
- adoption by unsavoury types and 'chavs' devalued the brand
- predominance of counterfeit items

19

Exploring Evidence of Your Future Success

Evidence helps prove the viability of your idea. Imagine what your business will be like if your vision succeeds. Then think about what evidence will provide proof of its success. Use Worksheet 02b: Evidence Modelling to help you explore these points. Imagine the future of your business and describe in words and images its consequences. Use as many stickies as you need to answer the four questions. Before you start, ask yourself:

'If my business becomes successful in the future, how will I recognise it?'

If you're pioneering a new way of doing something, what would its impact be on the environment? How might your business affect society or the industry you work within?

In answering the questions about your business (what will it enhance, what will it replace, what will it revive and what will be the backlash), try imagining the consequences from a number of viewpoints, such as:

- The wider world (think as big as possible)
- Your particular industry/field (e.g. how it might impact on current industry practices)
- Your customers (what benefits will it bring them)
- On you (what impact could it have on your work/life?).

20

EVIDENCE MODELLING

The example below shows how an entrepreneur has used the Evidence Model to help explore the consequences of their business.

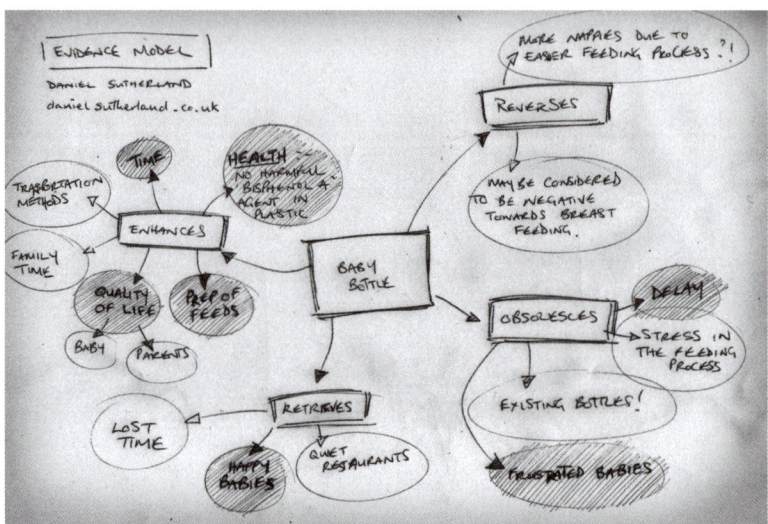

FUTURE EVIDENCE

Once you've imagined the future of your business, it helps to construct evidence of its success.

For example, if you're creating a new transport service based around car sharing, what would its impact be on the insurance industry? You could create an insurance quotation from an insurance firm showing how four people will be listed on one insurance premium.

Try creating your own persuasive visual argument to support your idea. This could become an important sales tool for you in the future. Having a compelling argument can attract collaborators to help implement your vision, as well as arousing the desire in your customers for your product or service.

Below are examples of Future Evidence created by entrepreneurs who have used this process.

You could use your Future Evidence not only in planning your business, but also as a way of communicating your idea to potential supporters in combination with the more standard business predictions, such as cash flow forecasts. After all a cash flow is just another type of prediction: one that shows you know how much it will cost to make your business idea happen, how much you will need to charge, and how many you will have to sell.

22

SWOT ANALYSIS

Now that you have explored what your business might look like if it were to become very successful, you should do a SWOT analysis. SWOT stands for strengths, weaknesses, opportunities and threats. By identifying these aspects of your company, a SWOT analysis allows you to evaluate its strategic position. Strengths and weaknesses are both internal factors that are controllable, whereas the opportunities and threats are generally affected by external factors that you can't control.

One of the main reasons for doing a SWOT analysis is to help you to turn perceived company weaknesses into strengths, and threats into opportunities.

Here's what a SWOT analysis might look like:

STRENGTHS
(Internal Factors)
- Well educated team
- Original Patented idea

WEAKNESSES
(Internal Factors)
- Low market profile
- Lack of turnover
- No key customer

OPPORTUNITIES
(External Factors)
- Clear market opportunity
- Competitor product at mature stage of cycle

THREATS
(External Factors)
- New competitors entering market
- Window of opportunity before product is superseded

BEFORE WE MOVE ON

You've used a number of exercises to help give shape to your idea in terms of its business potential. To summarise what we've gone through so far:

- There are some basic business facts that will help you succeed in your business. The key one is engaging with your customers to understand their needs.

- You have guidance on identifying, protecting and maximising your IP.

- Your personal values, energy and ambitions will help define your working environment, and will make the difference between your business and others.

- A business idea that balances passions, talents and economic drive will enhance the chances of success and sustainability.

- A mission statement summarises the aspirations for your business and can help guide the activities of your business.

- Through Evidence Modelling you've explored what your business might look like if it's very successful. This helps you to interrogate your vision and to define and communicate your idea so other people can understand and input into it.

- You've created Future Evidence to illustrate what success will look like for you.

- A SWOT analysis has allowed you to look at the strategic positioning of your company, and to identify possible weaknesses and threats as well as strengths and opportunities.

BEFORE WE MOVE ON

The next step is to define your milestones (your goals and objectives) and clarify how you'll develop your business.

In handbook 03 / **Choosing your path** we look at:

- Identifying your customers
- Building the various relationships you'll want to help your business move forward
- Detailing how your business will work to deliver your products or services.

Notes